Contents

Badger
L E A R N I N G

Vocabulary

blisters	infected
buboes	pneumonic plague
bubonic plague	pock mark
disease	vaccination

PLAGUE AND POX

JOHN TOWNSEND

WOW! facts

Badger Publishing Limited
Oldmedow Road,
Hardwick Industrial Estate,
King's Lynn PE30 4JJ
Telephone: 01438 791037

www.badgerlearning.co.uk

2 4 6 8 10 9 7 5 3

Plague and Pox ISBN 978-1-78464-028-6

Publisher: Susan Ross
Senior Editor: Danny Pearson
Publishing Assistant: Claire Morgan
Designer: Fiona Grant
Series Consultant: Dee Reid

Photos: Cover image: AFP/Getty Images
Page 5: © Brain light/Alamy
Page 6: © Scott Camazine/Alamy
Page 8: © Serge Vero/Alamy
Page 9: © GL Archive/Alamy
Page 11: De Agostini/Getty Images
Page 12: © 19th era/Alamy
Page 13: © Pep Roig/Alamy
Page 14: Universal History Archive/Un/REX
Page 16: REX
Page 17: Karl Schoendorfer/REX
Page 18: © Noedelhap/iStock
Page 19: © Medical-on-Line/Alamy
Page 20: © Prisma Bildagentur AG/Alamy
Page 21: Print Collector/Getty Images
Page 22: © North Wind Picture Archives/Alamy
Page 23: © Everett Collection Historical/Alamy
Page 24: © Everett Collection Historical/Alamy
Page 25: © World History Archive/Alamy
Page 26: © Everett Collection Historical/Alamy
Page 27: © Everett Collection Historical/Alamy
Page 28: © dpa picture alliance/Alamy
Page 29: © BSIP SA/Alamy

Attempts to contact all copyright holders have been made.
If any omitted would care to contact Badger Learning, we will be happy to make appropriate arrangements.

Killer diseases

Tiny living things can get inside our bodies and make us ill.

Long ago people didn't know about germs. They thought illness came from evil spirits or bad air.

They didn't know many diseases are spread by people touching, sneezing or just being close to each other.

1. WHAT IS THE PLAGUE?

Plague is a disease that quickly spreads. It has existed for thousands of years.

It is spread by fleas that live on rats. One bite from a flea could infect you with the plague and you would die a horrible death.

Plague outbreaks

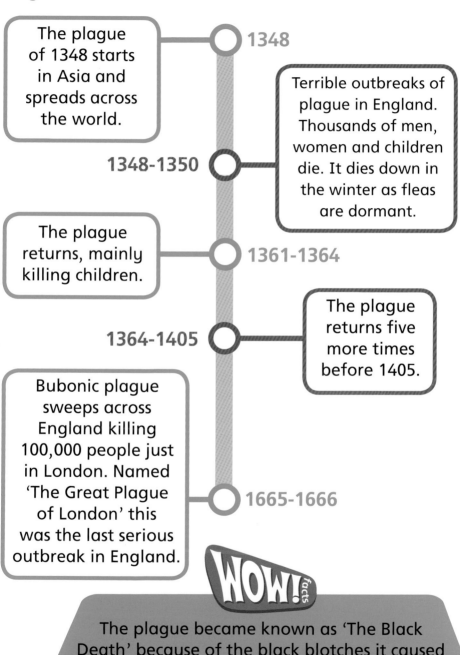

The plague of 1348 starts in Asia and spreads across the world.

1348

1348-1350 Terrible outbreaks of plague in England. Thousands of men, women and children die. It dies down in the winter as fleas are dormant.

The plague returns, mainly killing children.

1361-1364

1364-1405 The plague returns five more times before 1405.

Bubonic plague sweeps across England killing 100,000 people just in London. Named 'The Great Plague of London' this was the last serious outbreak in England.

1665-1666

WOW! facts

The plague became known as 'The Black Death' because of the black blotches it caused on the skin and its deadly effect on society.

Plague doctors

In the 1361–1364 outbreak of the plague there were special doctors who tried to help people.

But the doctors were scared of catching the plague so they wore special outfits to protect themselves. This was how a plague doctor looked:

WOW! facts

The bird-like beak was filled with nice smelling things to protect the doctor from 'evil' bad smells.

London's last plague

In 1665 the Great Plague of London killed almost 100,000 people in the city.

There were so many rats spreading the disease that in a few months it had killed two out of every ten people in London.

One year later there was a great fire in London that destroyed most of the city.

One good thing was that the flames helped to kill rats, fleas and the dreaded disease itself.

How do you know if you've got the bubonic plague?

First of all you get:
- a headache
- fever
- aches at the top of the legs
- a white tongue
- a fast pulse

Three days later you get nasty bumps in the:
- neck
- armpits
- groin

The bumps are called 'buboes', which is where the name 'bubonic' comes from. Some of the bumps are the size of an egg and some are the size of an apple!

Next, you start bleeding under the skin. This causes purple blotches, which turn black and smelly.

Four to seven days after catching the plague, you are likely to die.

About 50-75% of people who caught it died.

2. HOW THE PLAGUE SPREAD SO QUICKLY

The plague spread quickly from one person to the next because many people lived in very crowded housing.

Rats were everywhere and so were fleas. When fleas hopped from rats to people, they passed on the disease.

One week after being bitten by an infected flea you could be dead.

In London they tried to stop the plague spreading.

If anyone was thought to have the disease they were boarded up inside their house so they couldn't get out.

Other members of the family couldn't leave the house so they would die, too.

Then after a week the house was broken into and the bodies were buried in mass graves.

Mad cures

People tried many ways to cure the plague.

- sitting in dung (many doctors believed bad smells could drive out the plague)

- sitting in a room between two huge fires

- filling the house with herbs

- washing yourself in vinegar

- cutting yourself to bleed away the fever

- drinking your own urine twice a day

None of them worked.

5. BRITAIN'S PLAGUES

Grim discovery

In 2014, workers laying a new railway in London dug up 25 skeletons of men, women and children.

They had found a mass grave from the 1350s. Tests on the bones showed they were from victims of the plague.

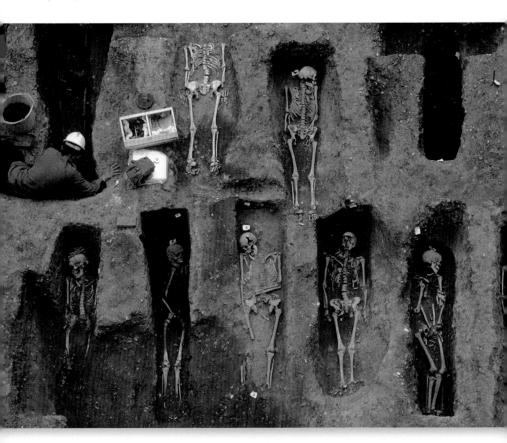

Scientists did tests on the teeth in the skulls.

They found out the victims had an extra deadly type of plague called pneumonic plague. Pneumonic plague attacked the lungs.

DNA showed the disease spread very quickly by sneezing. It passed from one person to another just by breathing in the germs. Victims died in days.

Scientists also believe there are many more skeletons in the ground nearby – perhaps as many as tens of thousands.

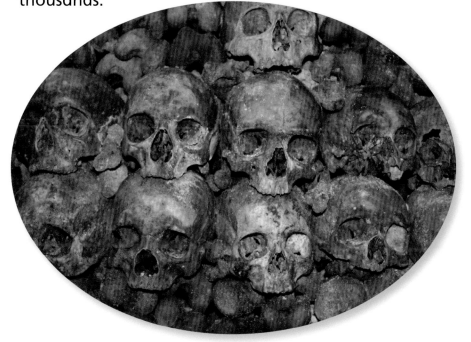

4. SMALLPOX

One of the biggest killers over the years has been smallpox. The smallpox virus spreads quickly.

How would you know if you had smallpox?

- First, you would get a fever and headache.

- Next, a rash would spread across your body, starting from your fingers and toes.

- In a few days, your body would be covered in pus-filled blisters and scabs.

- Then you might die.

Some people who caught smallpox got better. But their skin would have ugly scars, called pock marks, for life.

Eighty-five per cent of children under five years of age, who caught smallpox, died from the disease.

About 300 million people died from smallpox in the last century alone.

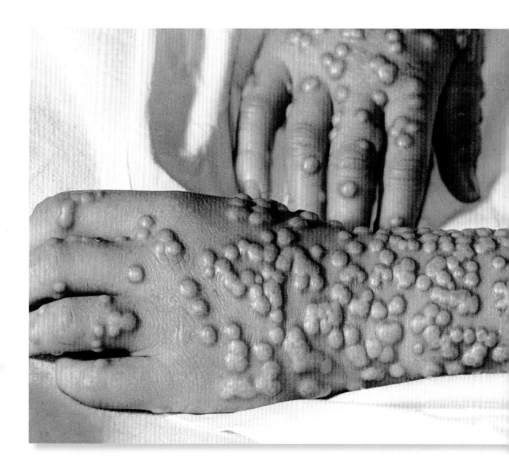

Mad cures

People tried many ways to cure smallpox. None of them worked!

- Heat and sweat. Patients were wrapped in blankets beside blazing fires.

- Bleeding. Leeches were put on a patient's skin to suck their blood.

- Patients were wrapped in red blankets in rooms with red walls, red curtains and red lamps.

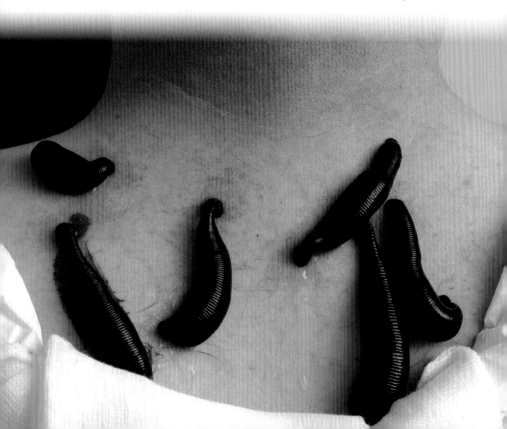

Queen Elizabeth I of England was given the red treatment when she caught smallpox in 1562.

She got better but her skin was left with bad pock marks.

She filled these with a sort of putty – made out of white lead and egg whites.

5. COWPOX

Farmers sometimes caught a virus from cows so it was called cowpox.

They got blisters on their hands but after a few days the blisters went and the farmer got better.

In 1796, a milkmaid called Sarah Nelmes caught cowpox after milking a cow called Blossom.

She went to see her doctor, Dr Edward Jenner.

He told her it was only cowpox and that she would get better soon. But Dr Jenner had noticed that people who caught cowpox didn't seem to catch smallpox, so he tried a test.

He took some of the pus from Sarah's cowpox blisters and injected it into an eight-year-old boy called James Phipps.

Can you guess what happened next?

James Phipps caught cowpox but soon got better.

But then Dr Jenner injected him with a small amount of the deadly smallpox virus.

James didn't catch smallpox!

This was because his body could fight the smallpox virus. When his body fought off the weak cowpox virus it had made it stronger to fight off the deadly smallpox virus.

Dr Jenner had found a way to stop people catching smallpox.

The Latin word for cow is 'vacca' so he called his new idea 'vaccination'. At last people could be protected against the killer disease.

WOW! facts

Dr Jenner took a big risk injecting James with smallpox but luckily it all worked out and later he bought a house for James to thank him!

6. A SMALLPOX-FREE WORLD

At first, other doctors did not believe in the idea of vaccination but after some time it was agreed that every child in the UK should be vaccinated against smallpox.

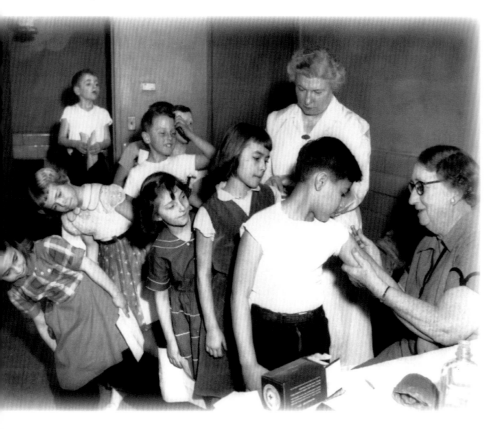

For years children across the world were vaccinated and in 1980 smallpox was the first disease to be wiped out forever.

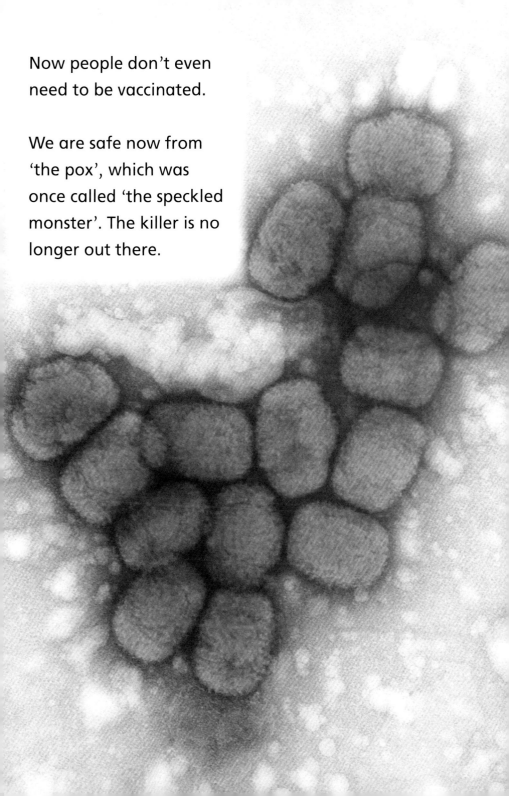

Now people don't even
need to be vaccinated.

We are safe now from
'the pox', which was
once called 'the speckled
monster'. The killer is no
longer out there.

Could smallpox come back?

It is very unlikely that smallpox could come back.

If the virus did break out again, the scientists are ready.
The USA and Russia still keep the smallpox vaccine
locked away in labs – just in case.

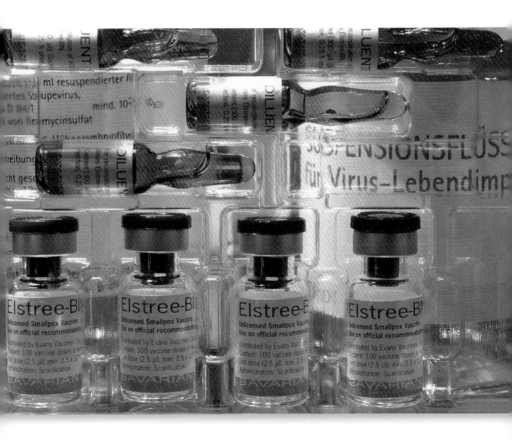

The 'plague' and 'the pox' killed hundreds of millions of people. Thanks to science, they are no longer dreaded killers.

Now, scientists are working on vaccines for other diseases to wipe them out.

AIDS research

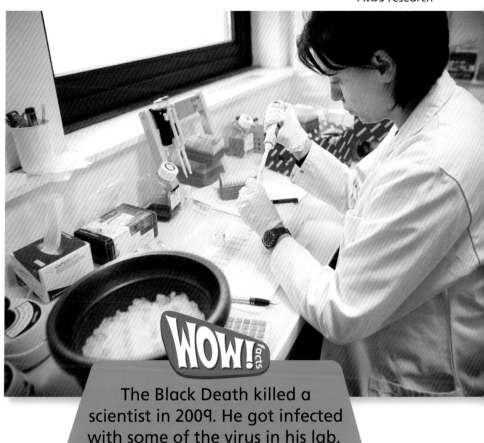

WOW! facts

The Black Death killed a scientist in 2009. He got infected with some of the virus in his lab.

Diseases today

Bubonic plague is still around today but there are only about 1500 cases each year across the world.

But deadly diseases can still strike:

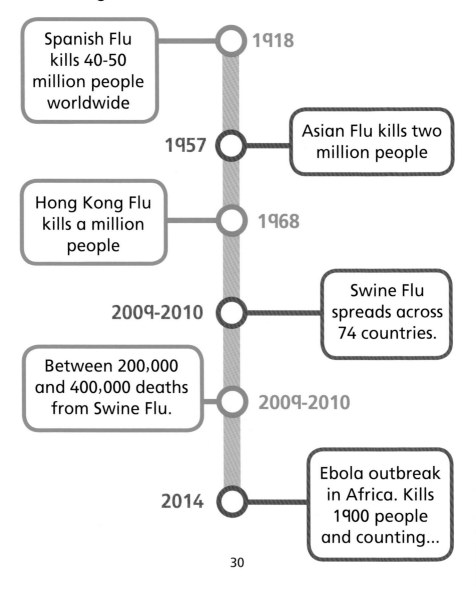

Spanish Flu kills 40-50 million people worldwide — 1918

1957 — Asian Flu kills two million people

Hong Kong Flu kills a million people — 1968

2009-2010 — Swine Flu spreads across 74 countries.

Between 200,000 and 400,000 deaths from Swine Flu. — 2009-2010

2014 — Ebola outbreak in Africa. Kills 1900 people and counting...

Questions

When was the Great Plague of London? *(pages 7 and 9)*

How does bubonic plague get its name? *(page 10)*

How long could it take to die after being bitten by an infected flea? *(page 13)*

Name one way people tried to cure the plague. *(page 15)*

Why is pneumonic plague so deadly? *(page 17)*

When was smallpox wiped out? *(page 26)*